ICONIC AMERICA

US ROUTE 66

BY MICHAEL DECKER

CONTENT CONSULTANT
Dr. Peter B. Dedek
Associate Professor in History, Texas State University
Author of *Hip to the Trip: A Cultural History of Route 66*

Cover image: Motels are some of the most famous features along Route 66.

Core Library
An Imprint of Abdo Publishing
abdobooks.com

abdobooks.com

Published by Abdo Publishing, a division of ABDO, PO Box 398166, Minneapolis, Minnesota 55439.

Printed in the United States of America, North Mankato, Minnesota
092019
012020

THIS BOOK CONTAINS RECYCLED MATERIALS

Cover Photo: Shutterstock Images
Interior Photos: Shutterstock Images, 1, 4–5, 14–15, 38 (middle), 45; Steve Lagreca/Shutterstock Images, 7, 43; Rainer Lesniewski/Shutterstock Images, 8; Currier & Ives/Historica Graphica Collection Heritage Images/Newscom, 12–13; Jose More/VWPics/AP Images, 19; AP Images, 21; LocalColor Photo/Alamy, 24–25; Andreas Feininger/The LIFE Picture Collection/Getty Images, 26; George Rose/Hulton Archive/Getty Images, 30; iStockphoto, 32–33; Michael Urmann/Shutterstock Images, 34–35; Ingus Kruklitis/Shutterstock Images, 38 (left); Phil Anthony/Shutterstock Images, 38 (right)

Editor: Maddie Spalding
Series Designer: Claire Vanden Branden

Library of Congress Control Number: 2019942103

Publisher's Cataloging-in-Publication Data

Names: Decker, Michael, author.
Title: US route 66 / by Michael Decker
Description: Minneapolis, Minnesota : Abdo Publishing, 2020 | Series: Iconic America | Includes online resources and index.
Identifiers: ISBN 9781532190940 (lib. bdg.) | ISBN 9781532176791 (ebook)
Subjects: LCSH: United States Highway 66--Juvenile literature. | Route 66--Juvenile literature. | Automobile travel--United States--Juvenile literature. | Migration, Internal--United States--History--20th century--Juvenile literature. | Scenic byways--Juvenile literature.
Classification: DDC 917.3--dc23

CONTENTS

CHAPTER ONE

ROAD TRIP

Abby is in the car with her family. They are in downtown Chicago, Illinois, at Grant Park. Tall buildings surround them. They are about to begin a long road trip. They see a sign for Route 66. The family will follow this route all the way to California. They will drive through prairies, mountains, and deserts.

Route 66 is a historic highway. It was one of the first and most traveled US highways. Over time, the road fell into disrepair. Today, other highways have replaced most of the original Route 66 road. But they follow the same route. The route runs through eight states: Illinois, Missouri, Kansas, Oklahoma,

A sign marks Route 66 in downtown Chicago, Illinois. From there, the route goes west.

GRANT PARK

Route 66 begins in the middle of downtown Chicago at Grant Park. Today, Grant Park is known for much more than being the starting point of Route 66. The park takes up more than 300 acres (120 ha) of land. It features sites such as the Art Institute of Chicago.

Texas, New Mexico, Arizona, and California.

Abby and her family are excited to see historic sites on their road trip. Many old motels, restaurants, and gas stations have been preserved along the route. The family heads out on the road. Abby looks out the window. She sees prairies and farmland after they leave Chicago.

The drive through Illinois takes most of the day. In the evening, they reach Missouri. The road signs change in Saint Louis. One reads "Interstate 44." Abby sees rolling hills and more farmland. They stay the night at the Wagon Wheel Motel. This motel opened along Route 66 in 1936. Abby and her family sleep in one of the motel's old cabins.

The historic Gay Parita station along Route 66 in Paris Junction, Missouri, no longer sells gas. Today, it sells food and other goods.

The next day, they continue their journey. They drive through part of Kansas and Oklahoma. This part of the route takes them another full day. Soon they reach Texas. They stop to eat at the Big Texan Steak Ranch, a historic Route 66 restaurant.

Over the next few days, the landscape changes as the family travels farther west. They see mountains in

MAP OF ROUTE 66

This map shows the path of the historic Route 66. Why do you think this path was chosen? Why do you think it was important for people to be able to access the West Coast?

New Mexico. They drive through the Painted Desert in Arizona.

Finally they drive into Santa Monica, California. Santa Monica is a coastal city near Los Angeles. Abby sees palm trees and sunshine. The family stops at Santa Monica Pier. They have reached the end of Route 66.

A HISTORIC ROUTE

Route 66 has a long history. The highway opened in 1926. It originally stretched from Chicago to Los Angeles. It was later extended farther west to Santa Monica.

Route 66 was not only an efficient way for Americans to get from the Midwest to California. It was also a scenic route. Along the route, drivers could see some of the country's most famous places. These included Lake Michigan in Chicago, the Ozark Mountains in Missouri, and the Grand Canyon in Arizona.

In the 1930s and 1940s, people opened more businesses alongside the road. These businesses included gas stations, cafés, motels, and trading posts. Small communities along the route became more popular as travelers stopped in these towns.

After World War II (1939–1945), people continued to use Route 66 to travel west. Thousands of families used the route to visit vacation destinations, such as Disneyland in California. But in the 1950s, construction began on other highways that followed similar paths to Route 66. More travelers began using these highways. By 1985, Route 66 was no longer part of the US highway system. But many groups across the country worked to keep the memory of Route 66 alive. Today, Route 66 looks much different than it did in the early 1900s. But it is still well traveled. Tourists and locals alike are drawn to historic Route 66.

PERSPECTIVES

MICHAEL WALLIS

Michael Wallis is a writer and historian. He has written a book about Route 66 called *Route 66: The Mother Road*. Wallis has a special connection to Route 66. He was born near the route in Saint Louis, Missouri. His family took road trips on the route. In a 2019 interview, he said, "I've lived in seven of the eight states it [Route 66] bisects, and as a reporter, I covered the stories of the road—the good, the bad, the ugly and the bittersweet. The road has always been part of my consciousness."

STRAIGHT TO THE
SOURCE

In 2019, journalist Hannah Lord wrote about Route 66 in an article for National Public Radio. She described the route's history and its importance. She wrote:

> *That skinny, two-lane highway has occupied the American consciousness since 1926. Its winding black pavement was the first road to link Chicago to Los Angeles, and over the years, millions of Americans looked for adventure, refuge and opportunity along its path. . . .*
>
> *Far fewer Americans drive cross country these days, but for millions of people, the song "Route 66" continues to conjure an image of riding westward with the top down along a two-lane blacktop looking for adventure.*

Source: Hannah Lord. "Route 66." *National Public Radio*. National Public Radio, May 6, 2000. Web. Accessed May 22, 2019.

What's the Big Idea?

Take a close look at this passage. How does Lord explain the route's significance? How is the route's history still visible today?

CHAPTER TWO

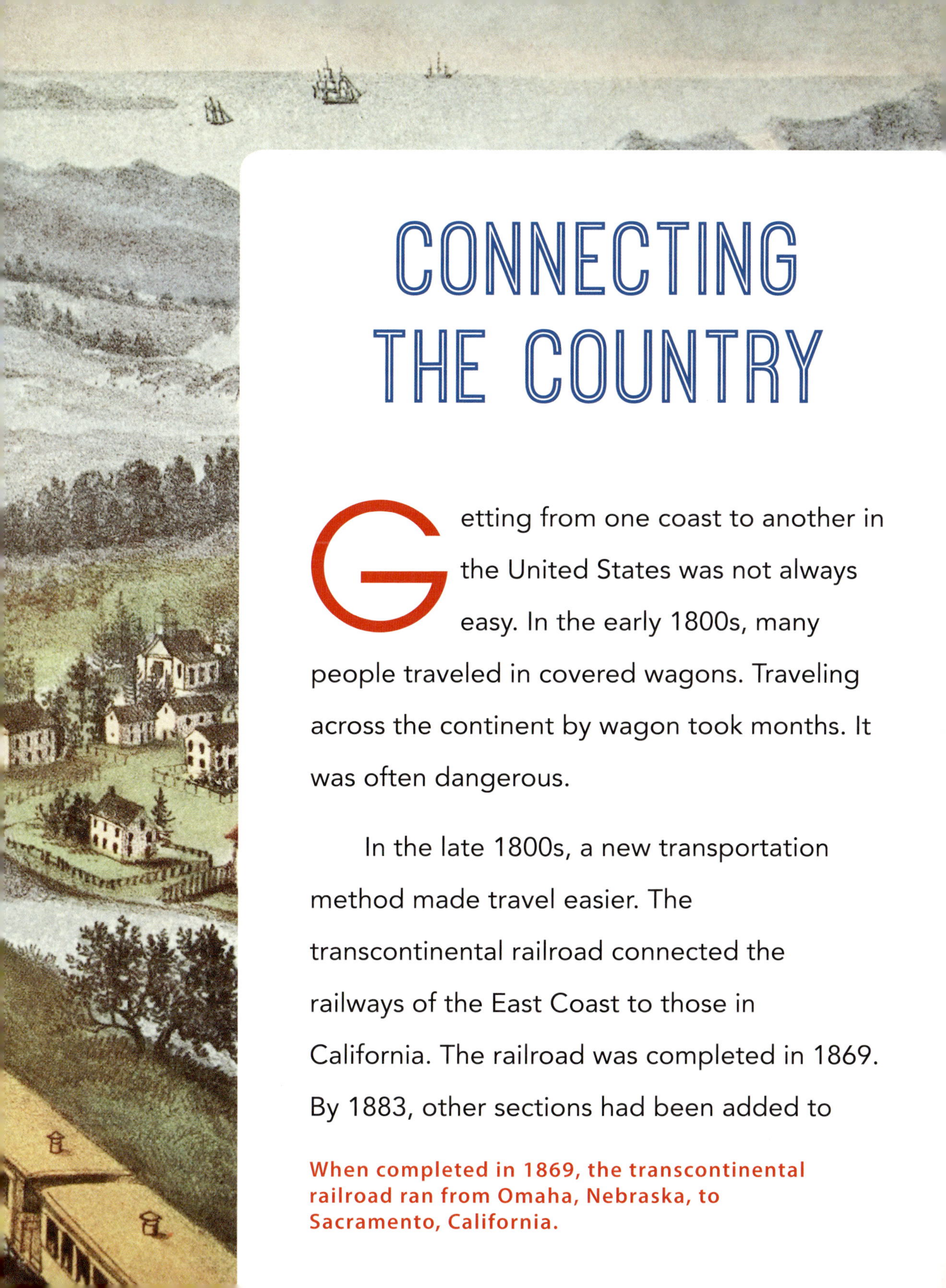

CONNECTING THE COUNTRY

Getting from one coast to another in the United States was not always easy. In the early 1800s, many people traveled in covered wagons. Traveling across the continent by wagon took months. It was often dangerous.

In the late 1800s, a new transportation method made travel easier. The transcontinental railroad connected the railways of the East Coast to those in California. The railroad was completed in 1869. By 1883, other sections had been added to

When completed in 1869, the transcontinental railroad ran from Omaha, Nebraska, to Sacramento, California.

One benefit of riding in cars instead of trains in the early 1900s was that it allowed travelers to set their own schedules.

the railroad. They connected New Orleans, Louisiana, to Los Angeles, California. Trains became the preferred method of travel. They were fast and safe.

In the early 1900s, cars became popular in the United States. Engineer and businessman Henry Ford introduced the Model T car in 1908. The Model T was

less expensive than other types of cars. As the price of cars went down, more people were able to afford them. Cars allowed families to set their own travel schedules and decide where they wanted to stop.

In the early days of car road trips, it was difficult to travel. There was no highway system. The dirt roads were often muddy and not well maintained. Many had large rocks or deep ruts. In the early 1900s, cars broke down more often than they do today. Travelers regularly had to stop to fix flat tires. Some cars got stuck in mud. Horses had to pull them out.

At the time, there were few gas stations or mechanical shops outside of cities. There were also few places along the roads where people could stop to eat or rest. But some gas stations and shops began to pop up along major roads in the 1910s. More people began to take road trips in their cars. They wanted to tour the country on their own and see important sites. But there still was no major road that connected many of the country's cities. Most people continued to rely on trains for cross-country travel.

In 1921, the US government passed the Federal Highway Act. This act set aside money to build highways. In 1925, a highway-naming system was created. Roads that ran east to west were given even numbers. Roads that ran north to south were given odd numbers.

Route 66 was named in 1926. The highway combined existing local, state, and national roads. Most of the road followed existing railroad tracks. The road was approximately 2,400 miles (3,860 km) long. Some of the existing roads were old. They were trails that had been created in the 1800s. Roads such as Ozark Trail and National Old Trails traced the paths early settlers took when

PROMOTION

In the 1920s and 1930s, promotional events brought attention to Route 66. A cross-country footrace was organized in 1928. Participants ran from Los Angeles to New York. They followed Route 66 from Los Angeles to Chicago. In 1932, Los Angeles hosted the Summer Olympics. The US Highway 66 Association put out an ad in the *Saturday Evening Post* magazine. The ad invited people to take Route 66 to Los Angeles to watch the best athletes in the world. Shortly after the ad ran, hundreds of people called the association's office requesting more information about the highway.

they traveled west. Route 66 followed these historic roads. Those who opened businesses along the highway hoped Route 66 would help bring in more customers.

EARLY HISTORY

The US Highway 66 Association helped spread the word about Route 66 in the 1930s. The association advertised the highway as the shortest and most scenic route from Chicago to Los Angeles. Other major routes were less direct.

The ads worked. Soon many people began to travel on Route 66. People opened more businesses along the highway. Hotels, gas stations, and other businesses popped up in the 1930s.

Each state that Route 66 ran through was in charge of fixing its section of the road. Some states had enough money to do this, but others did not. Many of the original roads were gravel or dirt. They were often in poor shape. In 1933, the US government began to help

In the 1930s, more gas stations opened along Route 66. The Standard Oil Gas Station opened in Odell, Illinois, in 1932.

states maintain the highway. The highway was not fully paved until 1938.

More companies began to use trucks to ship items across the country in the '30s. Truck drivers enjoyed Route 66. It was flatter than other highways. The southern states typically had nice weather. From 1931 to 1941, the number of trucks driving between Chicago and Saint Louis along Route 66 jumped from 1,500 per day to 7,500 per day.

HEADING WEST

Many people used Route 66 to head west. They wanted to find new opportunities in states such as California and Arizona. Throughout the 1930s, approximately 210,000 people moved from Oklahoma to California. They were trying to escape the Dust Bowl. The Dust Bowl happened when a major drought hit the middle of the country. It affected parts of Colorado, Kansas, Texas, Oklahoma, and New Mexico. Winds whipped through the dry plains, picking up dust. These dust storms were severe. They killed livestock and even people.

Other extreme weather and events also affected the Dust Bowl region and nearby areas. When these places did receive rain, the rain often caused flooding. Meanwhile, swarms of grasshoppers destroyed crops in the Midwest. These swarms were called plagues.

Crops failed from the drought, dust storms, and plagues. Many families lost their farms. Some people headed west to find new jobs.

Some people called dust storms "black blizzards."

At the same time, many Americans were struggling to make a living. The US economy had crashed in 1929. As a result, many people lost their jobs. This period was called the Great Depression.

In 1933, President Franklin D. Roosevelt created a series of programs called the New Deal.

These programs helped create jobs. Many of these jobs involved construction and road maintenance. From 1933 to 1938, thousands of men were employed to help pave and improve Route 66.

PERSPECTIVES

THE MOTHER ROAD

In 1939, author John Steinbeck's book *The Grapes of Wrath* was published. This book contains one of the most well-known references to Route 66. The book is set in Oklahoma during the Great Depression. A family moves west to escape the Dust Bowl. They travel along Route 66. In the book, Steinbeck called the highway the "Mother Road." He writes that the road is a home for those escaping the Dust Bowl. It is also a chance at a new life.

The Great Depression ended in the late 1930s. World War II broke out in 1939. The United States joined the war two years later. The US military used Route 66 to transport supplies. Military recruits used the route to get to training bases in California. The US government invested more money to help maintain the highway.

STRAIGHT TO THE SOURCE

In 1977, writer Thomas W. Pew Jr. wrote about Route 66 and the Dust Bowl for *American Heritage* magazine. He traveled along parts of the route. He wrote:

> *Along the old sections of Route 66 that pass through the Dust Bowl counties of Oklahoma and through the panhandle of Texas, the hills and flats are green with trees and native grass now. The restored land, after forty years of rest . . . has forgotten the spasm of drought and dust accompanied by plagues of bugs and periodic floods that expelled its bewildered tenants. But the old householders from this land—those who survived with their wits and lungs intact, and those who endured pulverizing poverty . . . cannot forget.*

Source: Thomas W. Pew Jr. "Route 66: Ghost Road of Okies." *American Heritage*. American Heritage, August 1977. Web. Accessed May 23, 2019.

Consider Your Audience

Adapt this passage for a different audience, such as your friends. Write a blog post conveying this same information for the new audience. How does your post differ from the original text and why?

CHAPTER THREE

NEW DEVELOPMENTS

After World War II, Route 66 became more popular than ever. Many Americans moved west to find new jobs. Thousands of soldiers had come west to prepare for the war. They settled in western states after the war ended. The populations of the states along the route increased dramatically.

Many people also used Route 66 to explore the country. The route provided access to national parks and historic sites. Families traveled along Route 66 on vacations.

El Rancho Hotel in Gallup, New Mexico, is a Route 66 landmark. It originally opened in 1936.

Cars drive along the stretch of Route 66 that runs through Seligman, Arizona, in 1947.

In the 1940s and 1950s, businesses along Route 66 continued to thrive. New businesses opened along the highway. Before the war, people had stayed in auto camps or tourist courts. Auto camps were places where people could park and camp in their cars. Tourist courts were places where people stayed in small cabins.

After the war, business owners opened motels along the highway. People could sleep in rooms with beds and bathrooms. Business owners often built these motels near gas stations and cafés. That way, people did not have to drive far to get gas or enjoy a meal.

Gas stations also changed during that time. They started out as small buildings with one or two gas pumps. They also offered other services such as tire repair. They later developed into larger businesses with more pumps and bigger garages.

ROUTE 66

In 1960, the television network CBS released a television show called *Route 66*. It aired from 1960 to 1964. It followed two men as they drove along different highways. Route 66 was one of the highways they drove on. The men met interesting people on their journey. They stopped at many sites along the way. *Route 66* showed what life was like in different US communities at the time.

REPLACING ROADS

Because Route 66 was well traveled, parts of the road became damaged over time.

Many trucks had transported supplies along the highway during World War II. They often carried loads of more than 30,000 pounds (13,600 kg). This weight and frequent use had not been good for the road. Parts of the road had many potholes. States did not have the resources to replace the road surface with stronger materials. Due to shortages during the war, Illinois and Missouri had replaced weakening steel bridges along the route with wooden bridges.

Parts of Route 66 were dangerous. The designers of the original highway tried to make it as straight as possible. However, some sections were very narrow. Others had sharp turns. This sometimes led to accidents.

The road's poor condition convinced President Dwight D. Eisenhower that updates to the US highway system were needed. Eisenhower signed the Federal Aid Highway Act of 1956. The act's purpose was to improve US highways. The act provided funds to construct a 41,000-mile (66,000-km) network of interstates. Interstates are highways that have four or more lanes. They have limited entrances and exits. They connect two or more states.

New interstates opened in the 1960s and 1970s. Interstate 40 was the first interstate to replace part of Route 66. It replaced a section of the road that went through Oklahoma, Texas, New Mexico, Arizona, and California. By the early 1980s, Interstates 55 and 44 were completed.

PERSPECTIVES

THE INTERSTATE SYSTEM

Many US highways needed repairs during World War II. But there was not enough money available to make all these repairs. Dwight D. Eisenhower had served in Germany in World War II. While there, he admired Germany's Autobahn highway system. He saw how fast people could drive and how safe the highways were. This later influenced his decision to sign the Federal Aid Highway Act of 1956. There were some superhighways in the United States at the time, such as the Pennsylvania Turnpike. These highways served as models when the interstate system was created.

Interstates made it easier for people to travel in and out of cities.

These interstates replaced other parts of the original Route 66. Interstate 55 ran between Chicago and Saint Louis. Interstate 44 ran between Saint Louis and Oklahoma City, Oklahoma. These interstates were modern, four-lane superhighways. Superhighways are highways with multiple lanes that are designed for high-speed traffic. The interstates were better designed for speed and safety than Route 66. The wider interstate highways made space for the growing number of Americans who used the highway system.

While some of the new interstates replaced parts of Route 66, others bypassed the original path. They no longer passed by some towns that had been on Route 66. Businesses in these towns lost customers. On the original route, drivers could easily enter the parking lot of a restaurant or motel from the highway. New interstates had exits, which made it more difficult to access most roadside businesses. As a result, businesses suffered.

EXPLORE ONLINE

Chapter Three explores the history of Route 66 after World War II. The article at the website below goes into more depth on this topic. How is the information from the website the same as the information in Chapter Three? What new information did you learn?

THE HISTORY OF ROUTE 66

abdocorelibrary.com/route-66

CHAPTER
FOUR

PRESERVING THE ROUTE

The new interstates quickly became the preferred roads. They were better kept than what was left of Route 66 and easier to drive on. In 1979, the American Association of State Highways and Transportation Officials ordered that Route 66 signs and markings along these interstates be removed. They said that these signs confused tourists.

By the early 1980s, only one section of the original Route 66 road remained. This section was in Williams, Arizona. In 1984, Interstate 40 replaced this final section.

The Route 66 Motoporium in Seligman, Arizona, displays old cars and historic Route 66 items.

Route 66 winds through many types of landscapes, including mountainous parts of Arizona.

In the 1980s, more Americans began traveling by airplane on their vacations. This meant that fewer people went on road trips. Attitudes about vacation and travel had also changed. In the mid-1900s, a major part of traveling was seeing the sights along the way. But by the time the original Route 66 had disappeared,

more people took trips with a single destination. They flew directly to that place. Even people taking road trips would stay on interstates rather than explore the countryside.

Cars were also designed better than they had been in the early 1900s. They did not break down as often.

People were able to drive for longer stretches without stopping. This was another reason businesses along the old Route 66 lost customers. Many businesses closed. Entire towns along the route were abandoned. They became ghost towns.

RESTORATION

In 1985, Route 66 was removed from road maps. It was no longer an official highway. The old Route 66 road had also lost some of its charm. But there were plenty of people who still wanted to preserve the highway's history. Many states put up signs that read "Old US 66" to mark the original route. Journalist Michael Wallis wrote a popular book about Route 66 in 1990. His book was called *Route 66: The Mother Road.* He wanted people to understand the highway's history and significance.

New Mexico senator Pete Domenici also wanted to educate people about Route 66. He traveled the route in 1990. He was saddened by all of the closed businesses along the route. He brought a bill to Congress to try to preserve the highway.

Congress passed Domenici's bill into law. The law was called the Route 66 Study Act of 1990. This act gave funds to the National Park Service (NPS). The NPS used these funds to study the remains of Route 66. It looked at how the route could be preserved and improved. Domenici hoped the improvements would attract more tourists to the route.

THE FATHER OF ROUTE 66

Many important figures are part of Route 66's legacy. Cyrus Avery was one such figure. He lived in Oklahoma in the 1920s, when construction on the route began. He participated in the Good Roads Movement. This movement called for better US roadways. He cofounded the US Highway 66 Association in 1927. As part of the association, he helped promote Route 66. He called the route the "Main Street of America." He helped convince people that the entire highway should be paved. For these reasons, he is often called the "Father of Route 66."

HISTORIC LANDMARKS

1909
Santa Monica Pier opens in Santa Monica, California.

1923
The Marsh Arch Rainbow Bridge opens near Riverton, Kansas.

1939
The Blue Swallow Motel opens in Tucumcari, New Mexico.

1949
The Cozy Dog Drive In opens in Springfield, Illinois.

1966
The Golden Driller statue is unveiled in Tulsa, Oklahoma.

The above timeline shows some of the historic landmarks along Route 66 that can still be found along the route today. It also shows the year each landmark opened. Why do you think these sites have been preserved?

Other government officials also worked to preserve Route 66. In 1999, President Bill Clinton signed the National Route 66 Preservation Bill. This bill gave funds to people, companies, and communities that wanted to honor the route's history. They promoted the route.

They also restored important historic sites along the route.

Outside of the government, other groups have formed in states where Route 66 ran. For example, the Route 66 Association of Missouri was founded in 1989. It promotes the section of the route that ran through Missouri and the businesses alongside it. The group also maintains many of the sites along the road. The Historic Route 66 Association of Arizona promotes the route too.

AN AMERICAN ICON

Many roadside attractions from the old days of Route 66 can be found along the route today. One historic place is the Gillioz Theatre in Springfield, Missouri. Since 1926, many famous musicians and comedians have performed at this theater. Another is the US Route 66–Sixth Street Historic District in Amarillo, Texas. This district was built in the 1920s. It contains many historic buildings.

PERSPECTIVES

THE *GREEN BOOK* PROJECT

In the 1900s, many restaurants and other businesses would not serve African Americans. Some white people attacked or even killed black people who tried to visit "whites-only" businesses. Victor H. Green attempted to help black people travel safely. Green was a black postal worker. He wrote a book he called the *Green Book*. It listed the places along highways such as Route 66 that were safe for black people. It was updated each year from 1936 to 1964. Today, Candacy Taylor documents the places featured in the *Green Book*. She says, "It [the *Green Book*] gave black people the freedom to experience America like everybody else."

Route 66 remains a popular road trip route today. Many people travel along the route by car or motorcycle. But other methods of traveling Route 66 are becoming more popular. In 2015, construction on a bike trail called the United States Bicycle Route 66 began. Once finished, this trail would follow the entire original highway route. It would allow cyclists to enjoy the sights of Route 66.

Route 66 has become well known

not only in the United States but also around the world. Travelers from countries such as Germany and Japan have come to the United States just to ride along Route 66. They see this highway as a symbol of adventure and freedom. Though Route 66 has changed over the years, it remains an American icon.

FURTHER EVIDENCE

Chapter Four explores Route 66's later history and legacy. Identify one of the chapter's main points. What evidence does the author provide to support this point? The website at the link below discusses popular attractions along the route today. Find a quote on this website that supports the main point you identified. Does the quote support an existing piece of evidence in the chapter? Or does it offer a new piece of evidence?

ROAD TRIP: ROUTE 66

abdocorelibrary.com/route-66

IMPORTANT DATES

1926
Route 66 opens.

1930s
The Dust Bowl ruins farmland in the Southwest. Many farmers who live in this region use Route 66 to head west to find new opportunities.

1941–1945
The US military uses Route 66 to transport supplies during World War II.

1945
World War II ends. More people begin to travel along Route 66.

1956
President Dwight D. Eisenhower signs the Federal Aid Highway Act of 1956. This act creates a network of interstate highways across the country.

1985
Route 66 is removed from road maps. It is no longer an official highway.

1999

President Bill Clinton signs the National Route 66 Preservation Bill. This bill helps promote the highway and restore old businesses along the route.

2015

Construction of the United States Bicycle Route 66 begins.

STOP AND THINK

Tell the Tale

Chapter One of this book discusses a family's trip on Route 66. Imagine you are making a similar journey along the route. Write 200 words about the cities and towns you would pass through on your trip. What else would you see along the way?

Dig Deeper

After reading this book, what questions do you still have about Route 66? With an adult's help, find a few reliable sources that can help you answer your questions. Write a paragraph about what you learned.

Say What?

Studying a historic travel route can mean learning a lot of new vocabulary. Find five words in this book you've never seen before. Use a dictionary to find out what they mean. Then write the meanings in your own words, and use each word in a new sentence.

You Are There

This book discusses how Route 66 changed after World War II. Imagine you are traveling on Route 66 during that time. Write a letter home telling your friends about your experience. Be sure to add plenty of details to your letter.

GLOSSARY

bill
a written document that may later become a law

drought
a long period of little rainfall causing a shortage of water

economy
a system in which goods and services are exchanged

highway
a major public road on which one can drive at high speeds, especially between cities

paved
covered by a material such as concrete or asphalt

pothole
a hole that develops in roads because of wear

scenic
having beautiful views or sights

transcontinental
something that crosses a continent

ONLINE RESOURCES

To learn more about Route 66, visit our free resource websites below.

Core Library CONNECTION
FREE! COMMON CORE MULTIMEDIA RESOURCES

Visit **abdocorelibrary.com** or scan this QR code for free Common Core resources for teachers and students, including vetted activities, multimedia, and booklinks, for deeper subject comprehension.

Booklinks NONFICTION NETWORK
FREE! ONLINE NONFICTION RESOURCES

Visit **abdobooklinks.com** or scan this QR code for free additional online weblinks for further learning. These links are routinely monitored and updated to provide the most current information available.

LEARN MORE

Lanier, Wendy Hinote. *Life during World War II.* Minneapolis, MN: Abdo Publishing, 2015.

Stewart, J. J. *Grand Canyon National Park.* Minneapolis, MN: Abdo Publishing, 2017.

INDEX

About the Author

Michael Decker has spent his career as a children's book author writing about various topics. He has also spent more than a decade coaching youth sports. He lives in Laramie, Wyoming, with his wife, three kids, and his dog, Emily.